SECRETS TO TURN FAILURE INTO SUCCESS

Learn to Bounce Back, Handle Failures Effectively, Set Achievable Goals, and Embrace Continuous Learning to Manage Stress

by

MAHUYA GUPTA

Copyright © 2024 by Mahuya Gupta

All rights reserved. No part of this book may be reproduced in any form without permission in writing from the author.

No part of this publication may be reproduced or transmitted in any form or by any means, mechanical or electronic, including photocopying or recording, by any information storage and retrieval system, or by email or any other means whatsoever without permission in writing from the author.

TABLE OF CONTENTS

Introduction 7

Rethinking Failure 9

    Failure as a Friend 9

    Changing Perspectives 11

    Cultural Views on Failure 14

    Eastern Philosophies: Embracing Failure as Growth 15

    Western Perspectives: Fear of Failure and the Pursuit of Success 15

    Indigenous Wisdom: Harmony with Nature and Adaptation 16

    Reflections and Insights 16

The Psychology of Failure 19

    Understanding Mindsets 19

    Fixed vs. Growth Mindset 19

    Stories and Analogies 20

    Emotional Responses 22

    Common Feelings Associated with Failure 22

    Techniques for Self-Compassion and Mindfulness 23

    Real-life Applications 24

    Overcoming Self-Doubt 25

    Addressing the Internal Critic 25

    Practical Steps to Build Self-Confidence 27

    Real-life Examples 28

Analyzing the Causes of Failure 31

    Identifying Patterns 31

    Common Causes of Failure 31

    The 5 Whys Technique 33

    Learning from Mistakes 34

    Performing a Personal Failure Audit 34

    Case Studies of Well-Known Failures Turned into Successes 36

    Taking Responsibility 37

    The Importance of Accountability 37

    Factors Within and Outside Our Control 38

Resilience and Bouncing Back 41

    Building Resilience 41

    The Science of Resilience 41

    Personal Stories and Practical Advice on Building Resilience 43

    Inspiring Tales 45

    Narratives of Individuals Who Overcame Significant Setbacks 45

    Drawing Lessons from These Stories 46

    Daily Resilience Practices 47

    Simple Habits to Cultivate Resilience 47

    Activities and Exercises for All Age Groups 48

Embracing Failure as a Learning Experience 53

    Turning Setbacks into Stepping Stones 53

    Techniques to Extract Lessons from Failures 53

    Personal Reflections and Inspiring Anecdotes 56

    Continuous Improvement 57

    How to Implement the Lessons Learned 57

    Encouraging Readers to Adopt a Mindset of Perpetual Growth 59

    Feedback and Adaptation 61

    The Role of Feedback in Learning 61

    Adapting Strategies Based on Experiences 63

Strategies for Resilience in the Face of Failure 67

Practical Resilience Techniques 67

Daily Habits and Practices to Build Mental Toughness 67

Sharing Personal Routines and Scientific Research 69

Community and Support 71

The Role of Social Support in Overcoming Failure 71

Encouraging Readers to Build Their Support Networks 72

Maintaining Motivation 73

Techniques to Stay Motivated After Setbacks 73

Overcoming Fear and Taking Action 77

Fear as a Barrier 77

Discussing Common Fears Related to Failure 77

Personal Stories and Humorous Anecdotes about Overcoming Fear 79

Taking the Leap 80

Practical Steps to Move from Fear to Action 80

Motivational Insights and Exercises for Readers 82

Celebrating Small Wins 83

Recognizing and Celebrating Progress 83

Sharing Stories of Small Successes Leading to Bigger Achievements ... 84

Conclusion: Embracing Failure for a Resilient Future ... 87

A Vision for the Future 87

Practical Advice for Maintaining Resilience Over the Long Term 88

Final Thoughts 89

Reiterating the Importance of Embracing Failure on the Path to Success 91

References 97

Disclaimer 99

About the Author... 101
May I Ask You For A Small Favor? 103
Other Books Written By The Author 105

Introduction

Hello, dear friends,

Imagine life as a long and winding journey. Along this path, setbacks and failures often appear like shadows, casting doubts and making us question our direction. It's completely natural to shrink back when faced with the sting of defeat, to see failure as an unwelcome guest in our quest for success. But what if I told you that these very setbacks, the ones we dread, could actually be the stepping stones to our most significant victories?

Welcome to "Secrets to Turn Failure Into Success." Together, we are about to embark on a transformative adventure—a journey where we'll not just talk about failure but embrace it with open arms. We'll challenge the conventional narrative that failure is a mark of defeat and discover how it can become a powerful catalyst for our greatest achievements.

Let me share a personal story with you, a moment that is etched deeply in my memory—a time when failure felt like a heavy cloud, obscuring all hope. I remember the disappointment vividly, the self-doubt that crept into my thoughts. It felt as if I was standing at the edge of a precipice, looking into an abyss. But in that very moment of despair, I stumbled upon a profound truth: failure, when seen through the right lens, possesses a unique and transformative power. It's a power that can propel us towards extraordinary growth and success, if only we learn to harness it.

This book is your invitation to embark on this journey of perspective shift. We'll explore how to see failure not as a foe to be feared but as a wise teacher, holding the keys to unlocking our true potential. Throughout these chapters, we will dive into the fascinating psychology of failure, uncover the reasons behind our setbacks, and discover the resilience needed to bounce back stronger than ever. We'll uncover the hidden gems of wisdom that lie within every setback, and together, we'll learn how to transform failure into a driving force for success.

So, buckle up for a journey that goes beyond clichés and ventures into the heart of personal development. This isn't just a book; it's a guide and a companion for all of us who dare to face failure head-on and emerge victorious.

Are you ready to redefine your relationship with failure? Join me as we delve into the transformative power of embracing failure and set sail towards unparalleled success. The adventure awaits—let's begin!

Chapter 1

Rethinking Failure

Failure as a Friend

Hello, dear friends,

Imagine sitting down with a cup of tea and reminiscing about your closest friends. We often think of our friends as those who cheer us on, stand by us in tough times, and celebrate our successes. But what if I suggested that one of your greatest allies in life could be something unexpected, something many of us shy away from? What if I told you that failure, yes, failure, could be one of our most insightful friends?

Let's take a moment to reconsider how we view failure. Traditionally, failure is seen as a shadow lurking in the background, waiting to pounce when we least expect it. It's often viewed as the end of the road, a full stop in our story. But what if failure was more like a wise old friend who nudges us back on track when we stray? What if failure was, in fact, a guide that shows us the right path by highlighting the wrong turns we've taken?

Let me share a story with you. There was a time in my life when I was deeply invested in a project, pouring all my energy and passion into it. I was confident that success was just around the corner. But despite my best efforts, the project crumbled. It was a colossal failure, and I felt as if the ground had slipped from under my feet. In the immediate aftermath, it was hard to see anything but disappointment. But with time, as the dust settled, I began to see the situation from a different angle. I realized that the failure was not just an end but also a new beginning. It forced me to reassess my approach, to learn from my mistakes, and ultimately, it set me on a path to a much more fulfilling endeavor.

You see, friends, failure is not our enemy. It's more like that candid friend who tells us the truth even when we don't want to hear it. It's the friend who gives us the tough love we need to grow. Failure teaches us humility. It shows us our limits and urges us to push beyond them. It makes us resilient and prepares us for the challenges ahead.

Consider the story of Thomas Edison, one of the greatest inventors in history. Edison faced countless failures before finally inventing the electric light bulb. He famously said, "I have not failed. I've just found 10,000 ways that won't work." Each failure was a stepping stone, bringing him closer to his success. Edison's story is a testament to the power of embracing failure as a friend. It's a reminder that every setback is an opportunity to learn, to adapt, and to move forward with greater wisdom and determination.

Let's also take a lighter approach and think of failure in terms of everyday life. Have you ever tried to cook a new recipe, only to end up with a culinary disaster? Perhaps you've burnt a cake or overcooked pasta to the point where it's unrecognizable. These moments, while frustrating, are also laughable. They remind us that failure is a part of the learning process. Each kitchen catastrophe teaches us something new, whether it's the importance of following a recipe or the need to set a timer. And often, these little failures make for the best stories and the most memorable lessons.

As we journey through life, it's essential to embrace failure not as a dreaded adversary but as a valuable companion. Failure, when viewed from a positive perspective, becomes a powerful teacher. It provides us with the insights and experiences we need to grow, to improve, and to ultimately succeed. So, let's welcome failure with open arms and see it for what it truly is—a wise friend guiding us toward our greatest achievements.

Changing Perspectives

Now that we've begun to see failure as a friend, let's delve deeper into how we can shift our perspectives to harness its full potential. Our society often glorifies success and stigmatizes failure, but scientific insights and personal growth theories suggest that failure is an integral part of the journey toward success.

Have you ever wondered why some people seem to thrive after setbacks while others struggle to recover? The answer lies in how they perceive failure. Research by psychologist Carol Dweck introduces the concept of the "growth mindset," a powerful idea that can transform our approach to challenges. A growth mindset is the belief that our abilities and intelligence can be developed through dedication and hard work. It's the understanding that failure is not a reflection of our limitations but a stepping stone towards growth and mastery.

Dweck's studies reveal that individuals with a growth mindset are more likely to embrace challenges, persist in the face of setbacks, and see effort as a path to improvement. In contrast, those with a fixed mindset view their abilities as static and often avoid challenges for fear of failure. This fear becomes a barrier, preventing them from taking risks and ultimately limiting their potential.

Consider the story of J.K. Rowling, the author of the Harry Potter series. Before she became one of the most successful writers in the world, Rowling faced numerous rejections from publishers. At one point, she was a single mother living on welfare, struggling to make ends meet. But she didn't let these setbacks define her. Instead, she viewed each rejection as a learning experience, a step closer to her goal. Her persistence and willingness to learn from failure eventually led to her unparalleled success.

Rowling's story is a powerful example of how changing our perspective on failure can lead to extraordinary outcomes. By adopting a growth mindset, we can transform our approach to failure and view it as a valuable part of our learning journey.

Another fascinating insight comes from the field of neuroscience. Studies show that our brains are wired to learn from mistakes. When we fail, our brain activity increases, and we are more likely to adjust our strategies and improve our performance. This phenomenon is known as "error-based learning," where our brain uses errors as feedback to enhance our learning and decision-making processes.

Think about it like this: when you play a game for the first time and lose, you analyze your mistakes, refine your strategies, and try again with better techniques. Each failure sharpens your skills, making you more adept at the game. The same principle applies to life. Each setback provides us with valuable feedback, helping us to refine our approaches and ultimately succeed.

Failure also teaches us resilience, a crucial trait for personal growth and success. Resilience is the ability to bounce back from adversity, to recover and keep moving forward despite challenges. It's the grit that keeps us going when the going gets tough. Studies by psychologist Angela Duckworth emphasize the importance of grit and perseverance in achieving long-term goals. Duckworth's research shows that individuals who persist in the face of failure are more likely to achieve their objectives than those who give up at the first sign of difficulty.

As we embrace failure and shift our perspectives, we start to see setbacks not as dead ends but as detours that lead us to our destination. We begin to understand that each failure is a lesson, a guide that directs us toward better choices and greater successes.

So, dear friends, let's take a moment to reflect on our own experiences with failure. Think about a time when you faced a significant setback. How did it shape your path? What did you learn from it? How did it contribute to your growth and development? By rethinking failure and changing our perspectives, we open ourselves to a world of possibilities. We transform failure from a source of fear into a powerful force for growth and success.

Let's embrace this new perspective with open hearts and minds. Let's see failure as the beginning of something greater, a friend who guides us through life's challenges and helps us uncover our true potential. Together, let's embark on this journey of growth and resilience, knowing that every failure brings us one step closer to our greatest triumphs.

By viewing failure as a friend and changing our perspectives, we unlock the doors to a life filled with learning, growth, and unparalleled success. As we continue our journey in the following chapters, we will explore the psychology of failure, analyze its causes, and discover the resilience needed to bounce back stronger than ever. But for now, let's pause and appreciate the wisdom that failure has to offer. Let's welcome it into our lives with gratitude and curiosity, ready to learn and grow from every experience.

Cultural Views on Failure

Examining How Different Cultures Perceive Failure

Failure, my friends, is a universal experience woven into the fabric of human existence. Yet, its interpretation and significance vary across cultures, shaping our attitudes towards adversity and resilience. Let us embark on a journey to explore cultural perspectives on failure, enriched by stories and reflections from around the world.

Eastern Philosophies: Embracing Failure as Growth

In Eastern cultures such as India, China, and Japan, failure is often viewed through the lens of growth and spiritual evolution. Concepts rooted in philosophies like Buddhism and Taoism emphasize the impermanence of success and the transformative power of setbacks. Failure is seen as a natural part of life's journey, offering valuable lessons in humility, resilience, and self-awareness.

Example: In Japan, the concept of "kaizen" advocates continuous improvement through small, incremental changes. Failure is not stigmatized but celebrated as a stepping stone towards mastery and innovation. Companies like Toyota exemplify this approach, where employees are encouraged to experiment and learn from mistakes to foster a culture of continuous improvement.

Western Perspectives: Fear of Failure and the Pursuit of Success

Conversely, Western societies often place a premium on success and achievement, with failure perceived as a setback to be avoided at all costs. The fear of failure can deter individuals from taking risks and pursuing ambitious goals, contributing to a culture that values perfectionism and external validation.

Example: In the United States, the entrepreneurial spirit celebrates risk-taking and innovation but also faces the pressure of high-stakes ventures. Silicon Valley is renowned for its "fail fast, fail often" mantra, where startups embrace failure as a necessary part of the learning process. Entrepreneurs like Steve Jobs and Elon Musk are celebrated not only for their successes but also for their resilience in overcoming multiple setbacks.

Indigenous Wisdom: Harmony with Nature and Adaptation

Indigenous cultures across continents, from Africa to the Americas, offer profound insights into resilience and adaptation in the face of adversity. Traditional knowledge systems emphasize harmony with nature and community support, viewing failure as an opportunity for collective learning and adaptation.

Example: Among the Maasai of Kenya and Tanzania, resilience is embodied in their pastoral lifestyle. Droughts and livestock losses are part of their nomadic existence, requiring adaptive strategies and communal resilience. Elders impart wisdom through oral traditions, emphasizing the importance of perseverance and unity in overcoming challenges.

Reflections and Insights

Dear friends, these diverse cultural perspectives on failure remind us of its profound impact on personal growth and societal resilience. Whether viewed through the lens of Eastern philosophies, Western ideals of success, or indigenous wisdom, failure serves as a catalyst for learning, innovation, and community cohesion.

Example: In my own journey, I have witnessed how cultural perspectives shape our response to failure. Growing up in India, I was taught that failure is not an endpoint but a stepping stone towards self-improvement. This belief encouraged me to embrace challenges with courage and resilience, knowing that setbacks are integral to personal growth.

As we navigate the complexities of failure across cultures, let us cherish the wisdom gleaned from diverse perspectives. By embracing failure as a universal teacher and catalyst for growth, we honor the resilience inherent in every individual and community. Together, let us reframe our understanding of failure, transforming setbacks into opportunities for innovation, compassion, and collective progress.

In the chapters that follow, we will delve deeper into the psychology of failure, analyze its causes, and explore strategies for resilience in the face of adversity. Join me on this enlightening journey as we unravel the transformative power of embracing failure on the path to success.

Chapter 2

The Psychology of Failure

Understanding Mindsets

Hello, dear friends,

Have you ever wondered why some people bounce back from failure with a renewed sense of purpose while others seem to crumble under its weight? The secret lies not in their circumstances, but in their mindset—the invisible lens through which they view the world and their place in it.

Fixed vs. Growth Mindset

Let's dive into the fascinating world of mindsets. Dr. Carol Dweck, a renowned psychologist, has illuminated this concept beautifully in her research. She explains that we can broadly categorize mindsets into two types: fixed and growth.

A **fixed mindset** is like a stubbornly closed door. It believes that our abilities and intelligence are set in stone, that we are either born with talent or we're not. People with a fixed mindset view challenges as threats, avoid risks, and dread failure because it feels like a permanent mark against their ability.

On the other hand, a **growth mindset** is like an open window, welcoming fresh air and new possibilities. It holds the belief that abilities can be developed through dedication and hard work. People with a growth mindset see challenges as opportunities to learn and grow. Failure, to them, is not a reflection of their innate worth but a step in the journey toward improvement.

To illustrate this, let's think about two students, Ramesh and Suresh. Both are faced with a difficult math problem. Ramesh, with his fixed mindset, believes that he's just not good at math. When he encounters the problem, he quickly gives up, thinking, "Why bother? I'm just not cut out for this." Suresh, however, has a growth mindset. He sees the challenging problem as a puzzle to be solved. Even if he struggles, he perseveres, thinking, "I might not get it right away, but with effort and practice, I can figure it out."

Over time, Suresh, who embraces challenges and learns from his mistakes, will likely improve and excel. Ramesh, who avoids challenges and gives up easily, will miss out on the chance to develop his skills. This simple analogy highlights the transformative power of our mindset.

Stories and Analogies

Now, let's bring these concepts to life with a few more stories. Consider the tale of Steve Jobs, the co-founder of Apple. Jobs was famously ousted from the very company he started. For many, this would be a devastating blow, a signal to retreat and give up. But Jobs viewed this failure through the lens of a growth mindset. He used it as a period of reflection and learning, eventually returning to Apple and leading it to become one of the most innovative companies in the world.

Or think about a young child learning to ride a bicycle. Each fall and scrape could be seen as a failure. But through the eyes of a growth mindset, each tumble is just a step closer to mastering the skill. The child learns to balance, to steer, and eventually to ride confidently, all because they didn't see their falls as a reason to stop trying.

These stories teach us that our mindset shapes our responses to challenges and failures. By embracing a growth mindset, we open ourselves up to continuous learning and limitless possibilities.

So, how can we cultivate a growth mindset in our own lives? It starts with being aware of our inner dialogue. When faced with a challenge, pay attention to your thoughts. Are they fixed and limiting, like "I can't do this" or "I'm not good enough"? Or are they growth-oriented, like "I can learn from this" or "With effort, I can improve"?

Shift your language from fixed to growth. Replace "I can't" with "I can learn." Replace "I failed" with "I'm learning." Embrace challenges as opportunities to stretch your abilities and grow stronger. Celebrate effort, persistence, and progress, not just the outcome.

In the journey of life, our mindset is the compass that guides us through the ups and downs. By choosing a growth mindset, we turn failures into stepping stones, challenges into opportunities, and setbacks into setups for greater success.

Emotional Responses

As we delve deeper into the psychology of failure, it's essential to acknowledge the emotional terrain we navigate when things don't go as planned. Failure is often accompanied by a whirlwind of emotions—disappointment, frustration, sadness, and sometimes even shame. Understanding and managing these emotions is key to harnessing the power of failure for personal growth.

Common Feelings Associated with Failure

Let's start by exploring the common feelings that accompany failure. Imagine, for a moment, that you've prepared meticulously for a job interview. You've researched the company, rehearsed your answers, and dressed in your best attire. But despite your efforts, you don't get the job. The sting of rejection is sharp. You might feel a deep sense of disappointment, questioning your abilities and self-worth.

Or consider a student who studies hard for an exam but doesn't score as well as expected. The immediate reaction might be frustration or self-doubt, a feeling of inadequacy that whispers, "You're not good enough."

These emotional responses are natural. They are part of the human experience. But how we deal with these emotions can make all the difference in our ability to bounce back and move forward.

Techniques for Self-Compassion and Mindfulness

One powerful approach to handling the emotional fallout of failure is practicing **self-compassion**. Dr. Kristin Neff, a leading researcher in this field, describes self-compassion as treating ourselves with the same kindness and understanding that we would offer to a dear friend in distress. It's about acknowledging our suffering without judgment and extending to ourselves the comfort we need.

Imagine if your best friend came to you, feeling crushed after a failure. You wouldn't berate them or tell them they're not good enough. Instead, you'd offer words of encouragement and empathy. You'd remind them of their strengths and reassure them that this setback doesn't define them. Now, apply that same gentle approach to yourself. When you encounter failure, instead of harsh self-criticism, practice speaking to yourself with kindness and compassion.

Here's a practical way to cultivate self-compassion. The next time you experience a setback, pause and take a few deep breaths. Then, place your hand over your heart and silently say to yourself, "This is a moment of suffering. Failure is a part of life. May I be kind to myself in this moment." This simple gesture can help you acknowledge your pain, recognize that failure is a shared human experience, and remind you to be gentle with yourself.

Another valuable tool is **mindfulness**, the practice of staying present and aware of our thoughts and feelings without getting swept away by them. Mindfulness helps us observe our emotional responses to failure without becoming overwhelmed or reactive.

Let's say you've just received critical feedback on a project. Instead of immediately spiraling into negative self-talk, take a mindful moment. Notice your initial emotional reaction without judgment. Acknowledge the disappointment or frustration you're feeling. Then, gently bring your focus back to the present moment and remind yourself that this feedback is an opportunity to learn and grow.

Incorporating mindfulness into your daily routine can be as simple as setting aside a few minutes each day to sit quietly and focus on your breath. As you breathe in and out, observe your thoughts and emotions with curiosity and without attachment. This practice helps build emotional resilience, making it easier to stay grounded in the face of failure.

Real-life Applications

To bring these concepts to life, let's consider the story of Sarah, a young entrepreneur. Sarah started her own business with high hopes and dreams of success. But after a year of hard work, her business didn't take off as expected. She felt a deep sense of disappointment and questioned her decision to start the venture.

Instead of succumbing to self-doubt and giving up, Sarah decided to practice self-compassion and mindfulness. She acknowledged her disappointment and allowed herself to feel her emotions without judgment. She reminded herself that failure is a natural part of the entrepreneurial journey and that it doesn't define her worth.

Sarah also used mindfulness to stay present and focused on what she could learn from her experience. She reflected on what worked and what didn't, and she saw this setback as an opportunity to refine her business strategy. With a kind heart and a clear mind, she was able to pivot her approach and eventually found success in her next endeavor.

Sarah's story illustrates how embracing our emotions with compassion and practicing mindfulness can transform our response to failure. By being kind to ourselves and staying present, we can navigate the emotional waves of failure and emerge stronger and more resilient.

Overcoming Self-Doubt

In our journey through the landscape of failure, there's one companion that often tries to hitch a ride: self-doubt. It's that pesky voice in our head that questions our abilities and undermines our confidence. Addressing this internal critic and building self-confidence are crucial steps in transforming failure into a stepping stone for success.

Addressing the Internal Critic

Self-doubt is like an overzealous security guard who questions every move we make. "Are you sure you can do this?" "What if you fail again?" These thoughts can be paralyzing, stopping us from taking risks and seizing opportunities. But here's the secret: the internal critic is not an accurate reflection of our capabilities. It's just a voice, and we have the power to change the conversation.

Let's start by recognizing that self-doubt is a natural response to stepping out of our comfort zone. It's a sign that we're pushing our boundaries and growing. Instead of fighting this voice, we can acknowledge it with curiosity and compassion. When self-doubt arises, try saying to yourself, "Hello, self-doubt. I see you're here because I'm trying something new and challenging. Thank you for your concern, but I'm going to keep moving forward."

Imagine a stage performer about to go on stage. The internal critic might whisper, "What if you forget your lines? What if you make a mistake?" Instead of letting these thoughts spiral into panic, the performer can acknowledge them, take a deep breath, and remind themselves of their preparation and passion for performing. By confronting the internal critic with calm and confidence, they can step onto the stage and shine.

Another effective technique is to challenge the validity of self-doubt. Ask yourself, "Is this thought based on facts or fears?"

Often, our self-doubting thoughts are rooted in fear rather than reality. By questioning their accuracy, we can weaken their hold on us and reframe our perspective.

For instance, if you catch yourself thinking, "I'm not good enough," counter it with evidence of your past achievements and strengths.

Practical Steps to Build Self-Confidence

Building self-confidence is like nurturing a plant. It requires patience, care, and consistent effort. Here are some practical steps to help you cultivate a strong and resilient sense of self-confidence.

1. **Celebrate Small Wins**: Confidence grows from recognizing and celebrating our successes, no matter how small they may seem. Each step forward, each task completed, is a building block for your self-esteem. Keep a journal of your achievements and review it regularly to remind yourself of your progress and capabilities.

2. **Set Realistic Goals**: Break down your larger goals into smaller, manageable tasks. Achieving these mini-goals will give you a sense of accomplishment and boost your confidence. As you tackle each task, you build momentum and reinforce your belief in your ability to succeed.

3. **Practice Positive Self-Talk**: Replace negative, self-doubting thoughts with positive affirmations. Instead of saying, "I can't do this," tell yourself, "I am capable and prepared. I can handle this challenge." Over time, this practice can reshape your internal dialogue and strengthen your self-confidence.

4. **Embrace Continuous Learning**: Confidence comes from knowing that you can adapt and learn from any situation. Approach each failure as a learning

opportunity. Ask yourself, "What can I learn from this experience? How can I grow?" By focusing on learning rather than perfection, you build a resilient and confident mindset.

5. **Surround Yourself with Supportive People**: Seek out a community of friends, mentors, and colleagues who uplift and encourage you. Positive relationships provide a safety net of support and remind you of your strengths when self-doubt creeps in.

6. **Take Care of Your Well-being**: Physical, emotional, and mental well-being are the foundation of confidence. Make time for activities that nourish your body and soul. Exercise, meditate, pursue hobbies, and ensure you get enough rest. When you feel good, you're more likely to face challenges with confidence and resilience.

Real-life Examples

Let's bring these steps to life with the story of Ravi, a young professional navigating the challenges of his career. Ravi often struggled with self-doubt, especially when faced with new responsibilities. He would second-guess his decisions and hesitate to take on challenging projects.

To overcome this, Ravi started celebrating his small wins. Each time he completed a task or received positive feedback, he took a moment to acknowledge and appreciate his efforts. He also set realistic goals, breaking down his larger projects into manageable steps, which gave him a sense of accomplishment and clarity.

Ravi practiced positive self-talk, replacing thoughts like "I'm not sure I can do this" with affirmations like "I have the skills and knowledge to handle this." He embraced continuous learning, viewing each mistake as a lesson rather than a failure.

Ravi also sought support from his colleagues and mentors, who provided valuable feedback and encouragement. He made time for self-care, engaging in activities that rejuvenated his mind and body.

Over time, these practices helped Ravi build a strong sense of self-confidence. He approached challenges with a positive mindset, embraced opportunities for growth, and thrived in his career.

Ravi's journey shows us that by addressing the internal critic and taking practical steps to build self-confidence, we can transform self-doubt into a powerful force for personal and professional growth.

As we conclude this chapter on the psychology of failure, let's reflect on the profound insights we've uncovered. Understanding the role of mindsets, managing our emotional responses, and overcoming self-doubt are crucial elements in navigating the journey of failure and success.

By cultivating a growth mindset, we open ourselves to endless possibilities for learning and growth. By practicing self-compassion and mindfulness, we can navigate the emotional waves of failure with grace and resilience. And by addressing self-doubt and building self-confidence, we empower ourselves to take bold steps towards our dreams.

Remember, dear friends, failure is not a destination but a journey—a journey filled with valuable lessons and opportunities for growth. As we continue to explore the transformative power of failure, let's embrace each setback as a stepping stone on the path to our greatest successes.

The road ahead may be challenging, but with the right mindset, emotional resilience, and unwavering self-confidence, we can navigate it with courage and grace. Let's embark on this journey together, embracing failure as a powerful guide and companion on our way to unparalleled success.

Chapter 3

Analyzing the Causes of Failure

Namaste, dear friends,

Life is a journey with many twists and turns, and along the way, we are bound to encounter failure. But instead of viewing failure as an end, let's see it as an opportunity to reflect, learn, and grow. In this chapter, we will explore how to analyze the causes of failure, identify patterns, learn from our mistakes, and take responsibility for our actions. By understanding the root causes of our setbacks, we can turn them into powerful catalysts for success.

Identifying Patterns

Common Causes of Failure

Failure can stem from a multitude of sources, and recognizing these common causes is the first step in transforming setbacks into stepping stones. Let's begin by discussing some frequent culprits that contribute to failure, enriched with real-life stories to bring these concepts to life.

1. **Lack of Preparation**: Many times, we underestimate the importance of thorough preparation. Consider the story of Rahul, a passionate musician who dreamed of performing on stage. He got an opportunity to play at a prestigious concert but failed to practice adequately. On

the day of the performance, he struggled to keep up, and his dream moment turned into a learning lesson about the critical role of preparation.

2. **Unrealistic Expectations**: Setting the bar too high without a realistic plan can lead to disappointment. Take the example of Priya, who started her own business with sky-high expectations. She aimed to become a market leader within a year but didn't account for the competition and market dynamics. When the business didn't take off as quickly as she hoped, she felt defeated. This experience taught her the importance of setting achievable goals and pacing her progress.

3. **Poor Communication**: Miscommunication or lack of communication can be a silent saboteur. Think of Arjun, a project manager leading a team on a crucial assignment. Due to poor communication, team members were unclear about their roles and responsibilities, leading to delays and misunderstandings. This failure underscored the necessity of clear and effective communication in any endeavor.

4. **Fear of Failure**: Ironically, the fear of failing can often lead to failure itself. Megha, a talented artist, was so afraid of critics that she hesitated to showcase her work. Her fear paralyzed her creativity and prevented her from pursuing opportunities. It was only when she embraced her fear and shared her art with the world that she began to succeed.

5. **External Factors**: Sometimes, external circumstances beyond our control play a significant role in our failures. The COVID-19 pandemic, for instance, disrupted countless businesses and careers. Many individuals, like Raj, found themselves facing unexpected challenges that required resilience and adaptability.

The 5 Whys Technique

To delve deeper into the root causes of failure, we can employ a simple yet powerful tool called the **5 Whys technique**. This method, popularized by Toyota, involves asking "Why?" five times in succession to uncover the underlying cause of a problem.

Let's illustrate this with a story. Imagine Kavita, an aspiring writer, who recently faced rejection from a publisher. She could have easily stopped at the surface level, attributing the rejection to bad luck or a tough market. But instead, she decided to use the 5 Whys technique to understand the true cause.

1. **Why was my manuscript rejected?**
   - Because the publisher found it lacked a unique selling point.

2. **Why did it lack a unique selling point?**
   - Because it was too like existing books in the market.

3. **Why was it like existing books?**
    - Because I didn't conduct thorough research on current market trends.

4. **Why didn't I conduct thorough research?**
    - Because I was focused on writing the story I wanted to tell without considering the audience's needs.

5. **Why was I focused only on my story?**
    - Because I underestimated the importance of aligning my vision with market demands.

Through this process, Kavita discovered that her rejection wasn't just about bad luck. It revealed a need for better market research and a more strategic approach to writing. By digging deeper with the 5 Whys, she gained valuable insights that would shape her future projects.

Learning from Mistakes

Performing a Personal Failure Audit

To learn from our mistakes, we must first understand them. A **personal failure audit** is a reflective exercise where we analyze past failures to uncover patterns and gain insights. Let's walk through this process with an example to make it engaging and relatable.

Meet Anil, a budding entrepreneur who faced multiple setbacks in his business ventures. Frustrated and demotivated, he decided to conduct a personal failure audit. Here's how he approached it:

1. **List Past Failures**: Anil started by listing all his business failures. This included unsuccessful product launches, partnerships that didn't work out, and missed market opportunities.

2. **Identify Common Themes**: He noticed recurring themes, such as poor market research, inadequate financial planning, and over-reliance on single sources of revenue.

3. **Analyze Contributing Factors**: For each failure, Anil examined the contributing factors. He realized that his enthusiasm often led him to rush into decisions without thorough analysis. He also identified a tendency to neglect contingency planning.

4. **Extract Lessons Learned**: Anil extracted key lessons from each failure. He learned the importance of comprehensive market research, diversifying revenue streams, and having a robust financial plan.

5. **Plan for Improvement**: Finally, Anil used these insights to create a plan for future ventures. He committed to more rigorous research, better financial management, and strategic planning.

Through this personal failure audit, Anil transformed his setbacks into valuable lessons. It helped him develop a more informed and strategic approach to his business endeavors.

Case Studies of Well-Known Failures Turned into Successes

Learning from others' mistakes can be equally enlightening. Let's look at some well-known figures who turned their failures into stepping stones for success.

1. **Thomas Edison**: Often cited as the epitome of perseverance, Edison faced countless failures in his quest to invent the light bulb. He famously said, "I have not failed. I've just found 10,000 ways that won't work." Each failure brought him closer to the successful invention that revolutionized the world.

2. **J.K. Rowling**: Before becoming a literary phenomenon, J.K. Rowling faced numerous rejections for her Harry Potter manuscript. Struggling with personal hardships, she persisted through failure and rejection. Her resilience paid off, and the Harry Potter series became one of the best-selling book series in history.

3. **Walt Disney**: Early in his career, Disney was fired from a newspaper job because he "lacked imagination and had no good ideas." He also faced bankruptcy with his first animation company. Undeterred, Disney continued to pursue his creative vision, eventually creating the iconic Disney brand that inspires millions worldwide.

These stories remind us that failure is not a dead-end but a detour that can lead to unimaginable success. By learning from their setbacks, these individuals turned their failures into fuel for their dreams.

Taking Responsibility

The Importance of Accountability

Taking responsibility for our actions is a crucial step in transforming failure into growth. Accountability means owning up to our mistakes, recognizing our role in the outcome, and taking proactive steps to improve. Let's explore this with an engaging analogy.

Imagine a cricket team that just lost a crucial match. The captain could blame the loss on the weather, the umpire's decisions, or the opposing team's tactics. But a true leader takes accountability.

They gather the team, analyze what went wrong, and identify areas for improvement. Maybe the batting strategy was flawed, or the fielding wasn't up to par. By taking responsibility, the team can work on these aspects and come back stronger in the next match.

In our personal lives, accountability works the same way. When we face failure, it's easy to point fingers and shift blame. But real growth happens when we look in the mirror and ask ourselves, "What could I have done differently?" Taking responsibility empowers us to make positive changes and learn from our experiences.

Factors Within and Outside Our Control

To effectively take responsibility, it's important to distinguish between factors within our control and those outside it. Let's break this down with a story.

Consider Ananya, who was preparing for a marathon. She trained diligently for months, but on the day of the race, she fell ill and couldn't perform at her best. Ananya could have blamed her failure solely on her illness, but she chose to reflect on the factors within her control. She realized that while she couldn't control getting sick, she could improve her diet and hydration strategies to boost her immunity in the future.

In any failure, there are elements we can influence and those we can't. By focusing on what we can control, we empower ourselves to take constructive actions. Here's a simple way to categorize factors:

1. **Within Our Control**: These include our actions, decisions, preparation, mindset, and effort. We can take responsibility for these and work on improving them.

2. **Outside Our Control**: These include external circumstances like weather, market conditions, other people's actions, and unforeseen events. While we can't control these, we can develop resilience and adaptability to navigate them.

To illustrate this further, let's look at the story of Sameer, a marketing manager who faced a major setback in a product launch. The campaign didn't resonate with the audience, leading to disappointing sales. Sameer could have blamed the market trends or economic conditions, but he chose to focus on what he could control. He reviewed the campaign strategy, gathered feedback from customers, and identified areas for improvement. By taking responsibility and focusing on factors within his control, he refined his approach and successfully relaunched the product.

As we conclude this chapter on analyzing the causes of failure, let's reflect on the powerful insights we've gained. By identifying patterns, learning from our mistakes, and taking responsibility, we can transform failure into a valuable learning experience.

Remember, dear friends, failure is not the end but a beginning—a beginning of a journey towards self-discovery, growth, and success. Each setback is a stepping stone, guiding us towards our true potential. As we continue on this path of embracing failure, let's approach each challenge with curiosity, resilience, and a commitment to learning.

The road ahead is filled with opportunities for growth and transformation. By understanding and analyzing the causes of failure, we equip ourselves with the tools to navigate life's challenges with wisdom and grace. Let's embark on this journey together, embracing failure as a trusted guide on our way to unparalleled success.

CHAPTER 4

RESILIENCE AND BOUNCING BACK

Namaste, dear friends,

Life, as we know it, is a series of ups and downs, victories and setbacks. In these ever-changing tides, one quality shines as a beacon of hope and strength—resilience. The ability to bounce back from adversity, to stand firm amidst challenges, is not just a skill but a lifeline. In this chapter, we will delve into the essence of resilience, understand its scientific underpinnings, draw inspiration from stories of those who have triumphed over trials, and explore daily practices to cultivate this invaluable trait.

Building Resilience

The Science of Resilience

To grasp the concept of resilience, let's first explore its foundation in science. Dr. Angela Duckworth, a renowned psychologist, has extensively studied this trait.

Her research reveals that resilience is a combination of passion and perseverance towards long-term goals. She describes this as "grit," a quality that allows individuals to keep moving forward despite setbacks.

Dr. Duckworth's studies highlight several key aspects of resilience:

1. **Passion and Perseverance**: Passion is our deep-seated enthusiasm for our goals, while perseverance is the tenacity to pursue them despite obstacles. Together, they form the bedrock of resilience.

2. **Growth Mindset**: Resilient individuals often possess a growth mindset—a belief that abilities and intelligence can be developed through effort and learning. This mindset fosters resilience by encouraging us to view challenges as opportunities for growth.

3. **Self-Control**: Resilience also involves self-control, the ability to regulate our emotions and behaviors in the face of adversity. This allows us to stay focused and calm, even under pressure.

4. **Positive Thinking**: Optimism plays a crucial role in resilience. By maintaining a positive outlook, we can better cope with stress and remain hopeful about the future.

Let's bring these concepts to life with a personal story. Meet Ramesh, a young man who dreamed of becoming a doctor. Despite his passion and dedication, Ramesh faced repeated failures in his entrance exams. Each setback was a blow to his confidence, but he refused to give up. Embracing a growth mindset, he saw each failure as a lesson and an opportunity to improve. He practiced self-control, managing his stress and maintaining a positive attitude. With relentless perseverance, he eventually succeeded, securing a spot in medical school. Ramesh's journey exemplifies the essence of resilience—passion, perseverance, and an unyielding belief in the possibility of success.

Personal Stories and Practical Advice on Building Resilience

Let's delve deeper into the personal journeys of individuals who have built remarkable resilience. These stories are not just tales of survival but powerful lessons on how to cultivate resilience in our own lives.

1. **Anita's Journey**: Anita was a young mother who lost her husband unexpectedly. Left to raise her two children alone, she faced immense emotional and financial challenges. Initially overwhelmed, Anita gradually found strength by focusing on her children and seeking support from her community. She embraced each day with hope and determination, building a new life for her family. Anita's story teaches us that resilience is often rooted in finding purpose and seeking support during tough times.

2. **Rahul's Challenge**: Rahul was a talented software engineer who faced a significant career setback when his company went bankrupt. Instead of succumbing to despair, Rahul saw this as an opportunity to start his own tech venture. He leveraged his skills, networked with industry professionals, and learned from his past experiences. Today, Rahul's startup is thriving, a

testament to his resilience and ability to turn adversity into opportunity.

3. **Maya's Recovery**: Maya, an athlete, suffered a severe injury that threatened to end her sports career. The road to recovery was long and arduous, filled with pain and uncertainty. However, Maya's resilience shone through. She set small, achievable goals, celebrated each milestone, and maintained a positive outlook. With time and perseverance, she not only recovered but also came back stronger, competing at a higher level than before. Maya's journey underscores the power of setting realistic goals and celebrating progress in building resilience.

From these stories, we can draw practical advice on building resilience:

- **Seek Support**: Surround yourself with a network of supportive family, friends, or mentors who can provide encouragement and guidance.

- **Focus on Purpose**: Find meaning and purpose in your actions, whether it's caring for loved ones, pursuing a passion, or contributing to a cause.

- **Set Small Goals**: Break down your larger challenges into smaller, manageable steps, and celebrate each achievement.

- **Stay Positive**: Cultivate a positive outlook, even in difficult times, by focusing on what you can control and finding silver linings.

- **Learn and Adapt**: View setbacks as learning opportunities. Reflect on what you can improve and adapt your strategies accordingly.

Inspiring Tales

Narratives of Individuals Who Overcame Significant Setbacks

Let's immerse ourselves in the inspiring tales of individuals who faced significant setbacks and emerged stronger, their stories serving as symbol of hope and resilience.

1. **Nick Vujicic**: Born without arms and legs, Nick Vujicic faced unimaginable challenges from the start. Bullied at school and struggling with depression, he could have easily given in to despair. But Nick chose a different path. He developed an incredible resilience, driven by a desire to inspire others. Today, he is a motivational speaker, author, and founder of Life Without Limbs, spreading messages of hope and perseverance worldwide. Nick's story is a powerful reminder that our limitations do not define us; our response to them does.

2. **Bethany Hamilton**: At thirteen, Bethany Hamilton's dreams of becoming a professional surfer were nearly shattered when a shark attack left her without an arm. Many would have given up, but not Bethany. With unwavering determination, she returned to surfing just one month after the attack. She went on to win national championships and inspire millions with her resilience and courage. Bethany's journey teaches us that

resilience is about rising above our fears and reclaiming our passions.

3. **Malala Yousafzai**: Malala Yousafzai's advocacy for girls' education made her a target of violence in her native Pakistan. Shot by the Taliban at fifteen, she survived and continued her fight for education with even greater resolve. Malala's resilience in the face of life-threatening adversity has made her a global symbol of courage and perseverance. Her story highlights the power of standing firm in our convictions, even when the odds are against us.

Drawing Lessons from These Stories

These narratives are more than just stories of overcoming adversity; they are rich sources of lessons on resilience. Here's what we can learn:

1. **Embrace Your Challenges**: Each of these individuals faced enormous challenges but chose to embrace them rather than be defeated by them. They turned their obstacles into opportunities to grow and inspire others.

2. **Find Your Inner Strength**: Resilience often comes from discovering and harnessing our inner strength. Whether it's Nick's refusal to let his disability limit him, Bethany's determination to return to surfing, or Malala's unwavering commitment to education, their inner strength propelled them forward.

3. **Stay True to Your Purpose**: Each story underscores the importance of having a clear purpose. Nick's mission to inspire, Bethany's passion for surfing, and Malala's advocacy for education provided them with a sense of direction and motivation to persevere.

4. **Seek Support and Inspire Others**: Resilience is not a solitary journey. These individuals sought support from their communities and, in turn, became sources of inspiration for others. Their resilience created ripples of hope and encouragement worldwide.

By drawing lessons from these inspiring tales, we can cultivate resilience in our own lives and face our challenges with courage and grace.

Daily Resilience Practices

Simple Habits to Cultivate Resilience

Resilience is not an innate trait but a quality that we can develop and strengthen over time. Let's explore some simple habits that can help us build resilience in our daily lives.

1. **Gratitude Practice**: Start or end your day by reflecting on things you are grateful for. This practice shifts your focus from what's going wrong to what's going right, fostering a positive outlook.

2. **Mindfulness Meditation**: Spend a few minutes each day practicing mindfulness. Focus on your breath and observe your thoughts without judgment. This can help reduce stress and improve emotional regulation.

3. **Physical Activity**: Regular exercise is not just good for your body but also your mind. Physical activity releases endorphins, reduces stress, and boosts mood, contributing to overall resilience.
4. **Journaling**: Keep a journal to reflect on your experiences, challenges, and emotions. Writing helps process your thoughts and gain insights into your responses to adversity.
5. **Self-Compassion**: Practice self-compassion by treating yourself with the same kindness and understanding you would offer a friend. Acknowledge your struggles without self-criticism.
6. **Goal Setting**: Set realistic and achievable goals. Break them down into smaller steps and celebrate each milestone. This builds confidence and a sense of accomplishment.

Activities and Exercises for All Age Groups

Resilience can be nurtured at any age. Here are some activities and exercises tailored to different age groups that can help cultivate resilience.

1. **For Children**:
   - **Storytelling**: Share stories of characters who face challenges and overcome them. Discuss what the characters did to persevere and how they can apply these lessons in their own lives.

- **Gratitude Jar**: Create a gratitude jar where children can add notes about things they are thankful for. This helps develop a positive mindset.

- **Mindfulness Activities**: Engage in simple mindfulness activities, such as focusing on breathing or observing their surroundings quietly for a few minutes each day.

2. **For Teens:**

- **Goal Mapping**: Encourage teens to set personal goals and create a visual map of the steps needed to achieve them. This helps in developing planning and problem-solving skills.

- **Resilience Journal**: Suggest keeping a journal where they can write about their challenges, how they overcame them, and what they learned from the experience.

- **Peer Support Groups**: Facilitate peer support groups where teens can share their experiences and learn from each other's resilience journeys.

3. **For Adults:**

- **Mindfulness and Meditation**: Practice mindfulness or meditation to manage stress and build emotional resilience. Guided meditation apps can be particularly helpful.

- **Physical Wellness**: Incorporate regular exercise into your routine. Activities like yoga, walking, or cycling can enhance physical and mental resilience.

- **Professional Development**: Engage in continuous learning and professional development. This keeps your skills sharp and fosters a sense of growth and achievement.

4. **For Seniors:**

- **Memory Sharing**: Encourage sharing and reflecting on life experiences and how they overcame past challenges. This can provide valuable insights and foster a sense of accomplishment.

- **Social Engagement**: Maintain social connections through clubs, volunteer work, or community activities. Social interaction is crucial for emotional well-being.

- **Creative Activities**: Engage in creative activities like painting, knitting, or gardening. These can provide a sense of purpose and relaxation.

As we conclude this chapter on resilience and bouncing back, let's remember that resilience is a journey, not a destination. It's about building the inner strength to face life's challenges with grace and perseverance. By understanding the science of resilience, drawing inspiration from others, and adopting daily practices, we can nurture this vital quality within ourselves.

Dear friends, each setback we encounter is an opportunity to build resilience and grow stronger. Embrace your challenges, seek support, and stay true to your purpose. Together, we can navigate the ups and downs of life with courage and wisdom, turning every adversity into a stepping stone towards success.

Chapter 5

Embracing Failure as a Learning Experience

Namaste, dear friends,

In the canvas of life, every thread of failure weaves into the greater design of our journey. Embracing failure as a learning experience is like turning the pages of a book where each chapter, no matter how challenging, brings us closer to understanding, growth, and success. Today, let us delve into how we can transform setbacks into stepping stones, continuously improve, and harness the power of feedback and adaptation.

Turning Setbacks into Stepping Stones

Techniques to Extract Lessons from Failures

Failures, my friends, are not the end of the road but the beginning of a new path. They are rich with lessons that can guide us towards greater wisdom and resilience. Here are some practical techniques to help us extract valuable lessons from our setbacks:

1. **Reflective Journaling**:
   - **What Happened?** Start by writing down the failure in detail. What exactly went wrong? What were the circumstances leading up to it?
   - **Why Did It Happen?** Analyze the root causes of the failure. Was it due to a lack of preparation, unforeseen circumstances, or perhaps a miscalculation?
   - **What Did I Learn?** Identify the lessons learned. How can you avoid similar pitfalls in the future? What new insights have you gained?

   Example: Consider the story of Arun, a young entrepreneur who launched his first startup with great enthusiasm but faced an unexpected market downturn. Instead of succumbing to despair, he took to journaling his experiences. Through this, Arun realized that he had neglected market research and competitor analysis. This insight helped him pivot his strategy and eventually build a successful business. Reflective journaling became Arun's tool for transforming setbacks into valuable learning experiences.

2. **Mindful Reflection:**
   - **Pause and Observe**: When faced with failure, take a moment to pause and observe your emotions without judgment. Mindful reflection allows you to gain clarity and perspective.

- **Ask Constructive Questions**: Instead of asking, "Why did this happen to me?" ask, "What can I learn from this?" and "How can I grow from this experience?"

Example: Meet Priya, who faced a major setback when she was not selected for a promotion she had worked hard for. Instead of dwelling on her disappointment, Priya practiced mindful reflection. She observed her feelings of frustration and acknowledged them. Then, she asked herself how she could use this experience to improve. This introspection led her to seek feedback, enhance her skills, and eventually achieve her career goals.

3. **Seeking External Perspectives:**

    - **Talk to Mentors and Peers**: Discuss your setbacks with trusted mentors or peers who can provide an objective perspective. They can help you see angles you might have missed.

    - **Constructive Criticism**: Be open to constructive criticism. Sometimes, others can see patterns or offer insights that are not apparent to us.

Example: Think of Raj, who experienced a significant financial loss in his business. Feeling overwhelmed, he sought advice from his mentor. The mentor provided a fresh perspective, pointing out areas where Raj could improve his financial management and risk assessment. This external perspective was instrumental in helping Raj recover and rebuild his business with stronger foundations.

Personal Reflections and Inspiring Anecdotes

Now, let me share with you some reflections and anecdotes that illuminate the power of turning setbacks into stepping stones.

1. **The Story of Thomas Edison:**

   - Thomas Edison, the prolific inventor, is often quoted for saying, "I have not failed. I've just found 10,000 ways that won't work." Edison's journey to invent the lightbulb was fraught with countless failures. Yet, each failed attempt was a stepping stone, bringing him closer to success. His story teaches us that perseverance and learning from each setback are key to achieving our goals.

2. **Anecdote from My Life:**

   - Let me recount a moment from my own life. I once attempted an English-speaking event where, despite my preparation, I faltered. The experience was humbling, and the initial embarrassment stung deeply. But upon reflection, I realized it was an opportunity to refine my communication skills. I sought feedback, practiced diligently, and returned stronger in my next endeavour. This personal failure became a stepping stone in my journey forward.

3. **The Tale of J.K. Rowling:**

   - Before becoming the beloved author of the Harry Potter series, J.K. Rowling faced numerous rejections from publishers. Each rejection letter could have been a nail in the coffin of her dreams. However, she viewed these setbacks as part of her learning process. Rowling's resilience and her ability to see each rejection as a lesson in perseverance eventually led to her extraordinary success.

- These stories remind us that failures are not barriers but gateways to learning and growth. By embracing setbacks and extracting their lessons, we pave the way for future triumphs.

Continuous Improvement

How to Implement the Lessons Learned

Learning from failure is only the first step. The true transformation occurs when we implement these lessons in our lives, fostering continuous improvement. Here are some practical steps to help us integrate the wisdom gained from setbacks:

1. **Create a Learning Plan**:

- **Identify Key Areas**: Focus on the specific areas where you need improvement based on the lessons learned from your failures.

- **Set Actionable Goals**: Define clear, actionable goals to address these areas. Break them down into manageable steps to ensure steady progress.

- **Monitor Progress**: Regularly review your progress and adjust your plan as needed.

Example: After a failed business venture, Anjali identified her lack of financial acumen as a key area for improvement. She created a learning plan to enhance her financial skills, setting goals to complete online courses, seek mentorship, and apply her knowledge in practical scenarios. This structured approach to learning helped Anjali rebuild her business with a stronger financial foundation.

2. **Adopt a Growth Mindset:**

   - **Embrace Challenges**: View challenges as opportunities to grow rather than obstacles to be feared.

   - **Learn from Criticism**: Be open to feedback and use it constructively to improve.

   - **Celebrate Effort and Progress**: Focus on the effort and progress made, rather than just the outcome.

Example: Suresh, a software developer, faced repeated setbacks in his coding projects. Instead of feeling defeated, he adopted a growth mindset. He welcomed challenges as opportunities to learn new coding techniques, sought feedback from his peers, and celebrated each small improvement. This mindset shift not only improved his coding skills but also boosted his confidence and resilience.

3. **Cultivate a Habit of Reflection:**

- **Regular Reflection**: Make it a habit to reflect on your experiences regularly. This could be through journaling, meditation, or discussions with a mentor.

- **Learn and Adapt**: Use these reflections to identify areas for improvement and adapt your strategies accordingly.

- **Commit to Lifelong Learning**: Embrace the philosophy of lifelong learning. Seek out new knowledge and experiences that can contribute to your personal and professional growth.

Example: Maya, a teacher, faced challenges in managing her classroom. She started a routine of daily reflection, noting what worked well and what didn't. Over time, these reflections helped her adapt her teaching methods, improve classroom management, and enhance her students' learning experience.

Encouraging Readers to Adopt a Mindset of Perpetual Growth

Continuous improvement is rooted in the mindset of perpetual growth—a belief that we can always learn, evolve, and become better versions of ourselves. Here's how we can cultivate this mindset:

1. **Stay Curious**:

- Approach life with curiosity. Ask questions, seek new experiences, and explore different perspectives.

- Embrace the unknown as a space for discovery and growth.

2. **Be Open to Change:**

- Recognize that change is a natural part of growth. Be willing to adapt and evolve in response to new challenges and opportunities.

- View change not as a threat but as an invitation to expand your horizons.

3. **Focus on the Journey:**

- Shift your focus from the destination to the journey. Celebrate the progress you make along the way, no matter how small.

- Appreciate the learning and growth that occur in each step of your journey.

4. **Seek Inspiration:**

- Surround yourself with people who inspire you. Learn from their experiences, perspectives, and wisdom.

- Draw inspiration from books, podcasts, and other resources that promote a growth mindset.

By adopting a mindset of perpetual growth, we can transform every experience, including our failures, into opportunities for learning and improvement.

Feedback and Adaptation

The Role of Feedback in Learning

Feedback is a crucial element in the process of learning from failure and achieving continuous improvement. It serves as a mirror, reflecting our strengths and areas for growth. Here's how we can effectively use feedback to enhance our learning:

1. **Seek Constructive Feedback**:

   - **Ask for Feedback**: Actively seek feedback from trusted sources, such as mentors, peers, or coaches. Ask specific questions to gain valuable insights.

   - **Be Open and Receptive**: Approach feedback with an open mind. Listen without defensiveness and consider the perspectives offered.

   Example: Priya, a writer, regularly sought feedback from her writing group. Initially, she found it challenging to hear criticism about her work. However, by remaining open and receptive, she gained valuable insights that significantly improved her writing skills.

2. **Reflect and Apply Feedback:**

   - **Analyze Feedback**: Reflect on the feedback received. Identify common themes and areas for improvement.

   Implement Changes: Use the insights gained to make meaningful changes in your work or approach. Implementing feedback demonstrates a commitment to growth and improvement.

Example: Ravi, a project manager, received feedback from his team regarding his communication style. Initially defensive, Ravi took a step back to reflect on the feedback. He realized that clearer communication could enhance team collaboration. Ravi adapted his approach, scheduling regular check-ins and fostering open dialogue. This adjustment not only improved team dynamics but also strengthened project outcomes.

3. **Provide Feedback to Others:**

   o **Constructive Criticism**: Offer feedback to others in a constructive and supportive manner. Focus on specific behaviors or actions and suggest ways for improvement.

   o **Encouragement and Recognition**: Acknowledge strengths and efforts alongside areas for growth. Positive feedback motivates individuals to continue their journey of improvement.

Example: Neha, a teacher, regularly provides feedback to her students on their assignments. She emphasizes both areas of improvement and commendable efforts. This balanced approach encourages students to strive for excellence while fostering a supportive learning environment.

Adapting Strategies Based on Experiences

Learning from failure is not a one-time event but an ongoing process of adaptation and refinement. Here's how we can adapt our strategies based on our experiences:

1. **Iterative Approach**:

   o **Experimentation**: Approach challenges with a mindset of experimentation. Test different strategies and solutions to determine what works best.

   o **Evaluate Outcomes**: Assess the outcomes of your efforts. What worked well? What could be improved? Use this evaluation to refine your approach.

Example: Arjun, an entrepreneur, launched a new product in the market but faced lukewarm response from customers. Instead of giving up, he adopted an iterative approach. Arjun gathered customer feedback, identified areas for enhancement, and iteratively refined the product based on user preferences. This adaptive strategy eventually led to increased customer satisfaction and sales.

2. **Flexibility in Approach:**

   o **Adapt to Changing Circumstances**: Recognize that circumstances may change, requiring flexibility in your approach. Be prepared to adjust your strategies in response to new information or challenges.

- **Embrace Agility**: Embrace agile methodologies that prioritize responsiveness and continuous improvement. This allows you to pivot quickly and effectively.

Example: Maya, a project manager, faced unexpected delays in a software development project due to technical issues. Instead of sticking to the original plan, Maya demonstrated flexibility. She reallocated resources, adjusted timelines, and collaborated closely with her team to overcome obstacles. This adaptive approach enabled Maya to deliver the project successfully within revised parameters.

3. **Learning from Successes and Failures:**

   - **Celebrate Successes**: Acknowledge and celebrate successes as opportunities for reinforcement and motivation.

   - **Reflect on Failures**: Similarly, reflect on failures to glean insights and identify areas for improvement. Treat each experience—whether success or failure—as a valuable learning opportunity.

Example: Anil, a sales manager, analyzed both successful and unsuccessful sales pitches. He identified common strategies that contributed to successful outcomes and areas where improvements were needed. By learning from both successes and failures, Anil honed his sales techniques and consistently improved his performance.

Dear friends, the journey of embracing failure as a learning experience is not just about bouncing back from setbacks but about bouncing forward with renewed wisdom and resilience.

By turning setbacks into stepping stones, implementing lessons learned, embracing a mindset of perpetual growth, and leveraging feedback for adaptation, we pave the way for continuous improvement in every aspect of our lives.

CHAPTER 6

STRATEGIES FOR RESILIENCE IN THE FACE OF FAILURE

Dear friends,

Life's journey is not without its challenges, and setbacks often test the strength of our spirit. Yet, it is precisely during these times of adversity that resilience shines brightest—a beacon of hope and inner strength. In this chapter, we will explore practical resilience techniques, the transformative power of social support, and effective strategies to maintain motivation in the face of failure.

Practical Resilience Techniques

Daily Habits and Practices to Build Mental Toughness

Resilience, my friends, is not merely a trait but a skill that can be nurtured and strengthened through daily habits and practices. Here are some practical techniques to build mental toughness:

1. **Morning Rituals for Resilience**:

   o **Gratitude Practice**: Start your day by expressing gratitude for the blessings in your life. This practice shifts your focus from challenges to the positive aspects of your journey.

- **Mindfulness Meditation**: Engage in mindfulness meditation to cultivate awareness and inner calm. This practice enhances resilience by promoting emotional regulation and reducing stress.
- **Visualization**: Visualize yourself overcoming challenges and achieving your goals. This mental rehearsal prepares you mentally and emotionally to face setbacks with resilience.

Example: Each morning, Meera begins her day with a gratitude journal, listing three things she is grateful for. This simple practice shifts her perspective and sets a positive tone for the day ahead. Combined with mindfulness meditation, Meera finds herself better equipped to navigate challenges at work and home.

2. **Physical Wellness for Emotional Resilience:**

- **Regular Exercise**: Incorporate physical activity into your daily routine. Exercise releases endorphins, improves mood, and enhances overall well-being.
- **Healthy Nutrition**: Fuel your body with nutritious foods that support brain function and emotional stability. A balanced diet contributes to physical and mental resilience.

Example: Rajesh, a busy professional, prioritizes his physical wellness by jogging every morning before work. The rhythmic motion and fresh air help clear his mind and boost his resilience for the day ahead. Coupled with a nutritious breakfast, Rajesh feels energized and ready to tackle challenges head-on.

3. **Stress Management Techniques:**

   o **Breathing Exercises**: Practice deep breathing exercises during stressful moments. Deep breathing calms the nervous system and promotes clarity of thought.

   o **Progressive Muscle Relaxation**: Engage in progressive muscle relaxation to release tension and promote relaxation. This technique enhances resilience by reducing physical and emotional stress.

Example: Priya, a student preparing for exams, uses deep breathing techniques to manage test anxiety. Before each study session, Priya takes a few minutes to breathe deeply, calming her mind and improving her focus. This proactive approach to stress management bolsters Priya's resilience during challenging academic periods.

Sharing Personal Routines and Scientific Research

The journey to resilience is enriched by personal stories and scientific insights that illuminate the path forward. Let us draw inspiration from both:

1. **Personal Routine: Anil's Resilience Journey:**
   - Anil, a middle manager in a competitive corporate environment, navigates daily challenges with a structured resilience routine. His mornings begin with a gratitude journal and mindfulness meditation, followed by a brisk walk to clear his mind. Throughout the day, Anil practices deep breathing exercises during high-pressure meetings, maintaining composure and clarity. By prioritizing physical wellness and stress management, Anil embodies resilience in action.

2. **Scientific Research on Resilience:**
   - Research studies, such as those by Dr. Angela Duckworth, emphasize the importance of grit and perseverance in building resilience. Duckworth's findings highlight how individuals with a growth mindset and resilience mindset are better equipped to overcome setbacks and achieve long-term success. By understanding the science behind resilience, we gain valuable insights into practical strategies for cultivating inner strength.

Dear friends, by integrating these practical resilience techniques into our daily lives, we empower ourselves to navigate challenges with courage and grace. As we embrace each day with gratitude, mindfulness, and physical wellness, we fortify our resilience for the journey ahead.

Community and Support

The Role of Social Support in Overcoming Failure

No journey is meant to be traveled alone, especially during times of adversity. Social support plays a pivotal role in fostering resilience and overcoming failure. Here's how we can harness the power of community:

1. **Building Support Networks**:

   - **Family and Friends**: Cultivate meaningful connections with family and friends who provide emotional support and encouragement during difficult times.

   - **Peer Groups**: Join peer support groups or communities of like-minded individuals who share similar experiences and challenges. These groups offer empathy, solidarity, and practical advice.

Example: Neha, a new entrepreneur, faced setbacks in her startup venture. She found solace and guidance through a local entrepreneur support group. Neha connected with fellow business owners who shared their own stories of resilience and offered valuable insights. Through mutual support and shared experiences, Neha felt empowered to persevere despite obstacles.

2. **Seeking Professional Support:**

   - **Therapeutic Guidance**: Consider seeking professional counseling or therapy to process emotions and develop coping strategies. Therapists provide a safe space for reflection, healing, and growth.

- **Mentorship**: Engage with mentors or coaches who offer guidance based on their own experiences and expertise. Mentors provide perspective, wisdom, and encouragement on your resilience journey.

Example: Rahul, a recent graduate navigating career uncertainty, sought guidance from a career coach. Through personalized coaching sessions, Rahul gained clarity on his career goals, identified strengths, and developed strategies to overcome setbacks. The mentorship provided Rahul with renewed confidence and resilience to pursue his aspirations.

Encouraging Readers to Build Their Support Networks

Dear friends, as we navigate the complexities of life, let us remember that strength is found not only within ourselves but also in the bonds we share with others. Here's how you can build and nurture your support networks:

1. **Reach Out and Connect**:

- Initiate conversations with family, friends, or colleagues. Share your challenges and successes openly, fostering mutual understanding and support.

- Attend social gatherings, community events, or workshops where you can meet new people and expand your network.

2. **Be Vulnerable and Authentic:**

   o Allow yourself to be vulnerable in sharing your experiences and emotions. Authenticity deepens connections and creates a supportive environment for growth.

   o Listen actively to others' stories, offering empathy and encouragement in return.

3. **Offer Support to Others:**

   o Extend a helping hand to those in need. Offer practical assistance, emotional support, or simply a listening ear.

   o By uplifting others, you strengthen your own sense of purpose and resilience.

Dear friends, by nurturing supportive relationships and seeking guidance when needed, we create a resilient community that uplifts and empowers each other through life's challenges. Together, we can overcome setbacks with resilience and forge a path towards greater fulfilment and success.

Maintaining Motivation

Techniques to Stay Motivated After Setbacks

Motivation, my friends, is the fuel that propels us forward on our journey, especially in the face of adversity. Here are practical techniques to maintain motivation after setbacks:

1. **Clarify Your Why**:

   - **Identify Your Purpose**: Reflect on your core values and aspirations. What drives you to pursue your goals despite challenges?

   - **Set Meaningful Goals**: Establish clear, achievable goals that align with your values and vision for the future.

   Example: Preeti, an aspiring writer, reconnected with her passion for storytelling after facing rejection from publishers. She clarified her purpose—to inspire others through her words—and set a goal to self-publish her first book. This sense of purpose and meaningful goal kept Preeti motivated and focused on her creative journey.

2. **Break Goals into Manageable Steps:**

   - **Create a Plan**: Break down larger goals into smaller, actionable steps. This approach makes progress tangible and manageable.

   - **Celebrate Milestones**: Acknowledge and celebrate each milestone achieved along the way. Small victories fuel motivation and momentum.

   Example: Rohan, a project manager, faced setbacks in completing a complex project on time. He created a detailed project plan with incremental milestones and deadlines. By focusing on completing each phase successfully, Rohan maintained motivation and ensured project progress despite challenges.

3. **Stay Positive and Resilient:**

   - **Practice Positive Self-Talk**: Challenge negative thoughts and replace them with affirmations of resilience and capability.

   - **Visualize Success**: Visualize yourself overcoming obstacles and achieving your goals. Visualization enhances motivation and reinforces belief in your abilities.

Example: Maya, a competitive athlete, sustained an injury that sidelined her from training. Despite setbacks, Maya maintained a positive mindset through visualization. She visualized herself returning to peak performance, focusing on the strength and resilience she had developed through previous challenges.

Dear friends, by clarifying our purpose, breaking goals into manageable steps, and cultivating a positive mindset, we sustain motivation on our journey of resilience. Let us embrace each setback as an opportunity to reaffirm our commitment to growth and achievement.

In conclusion, this chapter has explored invaluable strategies for building resilience in the face of failure. Through practical resilience techniques, the transformative power of community and support, and effective strategies to maintain motivation, we empower ourselves to navigate challenges with courage and determination.

As we continue our journey, let us remember that resilience is not the absence of adversity but the strength to rise above it, embodying the spirit of growth and resilience in every aspect of our lives.

Chapter 7

Overcoming Fear and Taking Action

Dear friends,

Fear, though a natural human emotion, often stands as a formidable barrier between us and our aspirations. In this chapter, we will delve into the common fears associated with failure, share personal stories of triumph over fear, explore practical steps to take decisive action, and celebrate the significance of small wins on our journey of growth and achievement.

Fear as a Barrier

Discussing Common Fears Related to Failure

Fear, my friends, manifests in various forms and can paralyze even the most courageous souls. Let us acknowledge and explore some common fears related to failure:

1. **Fear of Rejection and Criticism:**

    o Many of us hesitate to pursue our dreams for fear of facing rejection or criticism from others.

    o This fear often stems from a desire for acceptance and fear of failure in the eyes of others.

Example: Vandana, a budding artist, hesitated to showcase her artwork publicly due to a fear of critique. Overcoming this fear required courage and self-belief, ultimately leading her to exhibit her paintings at a local gallery. Vandana's bravery in confronting her fear of criticism allowed her artistic talent to flourish.

2. **Fear of Failure Itself:**

   o The fear of failing to achieve our goals can prevent us from taking the necessary risks and actions.

   o This fear may arise from a concern about setbacks, loss of confidence, or perceived limitations.

Example: Rahul, an aspiring entrepreneur, delayed launching his startup due to a fear of potential failure. However, he realized that every successful entrepreneur faced initial setbacks. By embracing failure as a learning experience, Rahul overcame his fear and took the leap to pursue his entrepreneurial dreams.

3. **Fear of the Unknown:**

   o Stepping into uncharted territory can evoke fear of uncertainty and unpredictability.

   o This fear often arises when we contemplate new opportunities or significant life changes.

Example: Sanya, considering a career change, experienced fear of the unknown as she weighed the risks and rewards. Through self-reflection and support from loved ones,

Sanya confronted her fear and embarked on a new career path. Embracing uncertainty as a catalyst for growth, Sanya found fulfilment and professional success in her new role.

Personal Stories and Humorous Anecdotes about Overcoming Fear

Dear friends, let us find inspiration in personal stories and humorous anecdotes that illuminate the journey from fear to courage:

1. **Anil's Leap of Faith**:
   - Anil, a software engineer, harbored a fear of public speaking for years. His anxiety about addressing large audiences hindered his professional growth. Determined to conquer his fear, Anil enrolled in public speaking workshops and joined Toastmasters. Through consistent practice and support from mentors, Anil transformed his fear into confidence. Today, he delivers inspiring presentations at conferences worldwide, inspiring others to face their fears head-on.

2. **Meera's Roller Coaster Ride:**
   - Meera, an adventurous soul, faced a fear of heights that kept her from experiencing thrilling roller coasters. Encouraged by friends, Meera reluctantly boarded a roller coaster at an amusement park. Despite initial apprehension, Meera found herself exhilarated by the adrenaline rush and conquered her fear of heights. Now, she embraces new challenges with enthusiasm,

proving that overcoming fear opens doors to joyful experiences.

3. **Raj's Comic Relief:**

   o Raj, a stand-up comedian, navigated stage fright early in his career. Before performing, Raj would envision the audience in their underwear—a humorous tactic to ease his nerves. Embracing laughter as a remedy for fear, Raj transformed stage fright into comic relief. His courage and comedic talent endeared him to audiences, illustrating that humour and resilience go together on the path to overcoming fear.

Dear friends, these stories remind us that courage is not the absence of fear but the willingness to confront and transcend it. By embracing challenges with resilience and humour, we cultivate the strength to pursue our dreams and aspirations.

Taking the Leap

Practical Steps to Move from Fear to Action

Courage, my friends, lies in taking bold steps forward despite our fears. Here are practical steps to overcome fear and embrace decisive action:

1. **Acknowledge and Understand Your Fears:**

   o Identify specific fears that hinder your progress. Understanding the root causes of fear empowers you to address them effectively.

- Journaling or discussing fears with a trusted friend can provide clarity and perspective.

Example: Priya, contemplating a career change, identified fear of financial instability as a barrier. By analyzing her financial situation and creating a contingency plan, Priya alleviated this fear and gained confidence to pursue her passion.

2. **Challenge Limiting Beliefs:**

- Examine beliefs that reinforce fear and self-doubt. Replace negative thoughts with affirmations of courage and capability.
- Engage in positive self-talk and visualize successful outcomes to cultivate a mindset of resilience.

Example: Rohan, aspiring to start his own business, confronted self-doubt about his entrepreneurial skills. Through mentorship and self-reflection, Rohan challenged limiting beliefs and embraced his potential for success. This shift in mindset empowered Rohan to take proactive steps towards launching his business venture.

3. **Take Incremental Actions:**

- Break daunting tasks into smaller, manageable steps. Each small action builds momentum and confidence towards overcoming fear.
- Celebrate progress and acknowledge your courage in taking each step forward.

Example: Maya, preparing for a competitive exam, initially felt overwhelmed by the extensive syllabus. By creating a study schedule and focusing on one topic at a time, Maya conquered her fear of failure. Each completed study session reinforced Maya's confidence and readiness for the exam.

Motivational Insights and Exercises for Readers

Dear friends, let us draw inspiration from motivational insights and practical exercises to conquer fear and take decisive action:

1. **Visualize Success**: Close your eyes and visualize yourself overcoming challenges and achieving your goals. Imagine the feelings of accomplishment and joy.

2. **Create a Fear-Conquering Mantra**: Develop a mantra or affirmation that reaffirms your courage and resilience. Repeat this mantra daily to reinforce positive beliefs.

Example Mantra: "I am courageous and capable of overcoming any challenge. With each step forward, I grow stronger and closer to my goals."

3. **Seek Support and Encouragement**: Share your fears and aspirations with supportive individuals who offer encouragement and constructive feedback.

Example Exercise: Write down your fears related to a specific goal or aspiration. Next to each fear, brainstorm actionable steps you can take to confront and overcome it.

Share your action plan with a trusted friend or mentor for additional support and accountability.

Dear friends, by acknowledging our fears, challenging limiting beliefs, and taking incremental actions towards our goals, we transcend fear and embrace the courage within us. Let us embark on this journey together, celebrating each step forward as a testament to our resilience and determination.

Celebrating Small Wins

Recognizing and Celebrating Progress

Dear friends, amidst the pursuit of our dreams, it is essential to pause and celebrate the significance of small wins along the way. Here's why celebrating progress matters:

1. **Fuelling Motivation and Momentum**:

    o Celebrating small wins reinforces positive behaviours and motivates continued effort towards larger goals.

    o Recognition of progress boosts confidence and reaffirms our capabilities.

    Example: Anjali, learning a new language, celebrated mastering basic conversational skills. Each milestone—holding a conversation, understanding nuances—fuelled her motivation to achieve fluency.

2. **Building Resilience and Perseverance:**

    o Acknowledging small wins cultivates resilience by affirming our ability to overcome challenges.

- Each achievement strengthens our resolve and prepares us for future obstacles.

Example: Aarav, an athlete recovering from injury, celebrated completing his rehabilitation program. Each milestone—increased mobility, strength—reinforced Aarav's determination to return to peak performance.

3. Fostering a Positive Mindset:

- Celebration fosters a positive mindset, shifting focus from setbacks to achievements.
- Gratitude for progress nurtures optimism and inspires continued growth.

Example: Diya, pursuing a writing career, celebrated completing her first manuscript draft. Each chapter written—characters developed, plot structured—sparked joy and fuelled her creative passion.

Sharing Stories of Small Successes Leading to Bigger Achievements

Dear friends, let us draw inspiration from stories of small successes that pave the way for greater achievements:

1. Neha's Artistic Journey:

- Neha, exploring painting as a hobby, celebrated her first exhibition at a local gallery. Each artwork sold—appreciation from patrons—emboldened Neha to pursue her passion full-time. Today, Neha's artistic journey—commissions, exhibitions—inspires others to embrace creativity.

2. **Karan's Entrepreneurial Spirit:**

- Karan, launching a tech startup, celebrated securing his first client. Each milestone—product development, customer satisfaction—propelled Karan's entrepreneurial journey. Today, Karan's startup—innovative solutions, market expansion—transforms industries.

3. **Riya's Academic Excellence:**

- Riya, pursuing higher education, celebrated achieving top honors in her class. Each grade earned—dedication to studies, academic accolades—nurtured Riya's intellectual curiosity. Today, Riya's academic journey—research publications, global recognition—ignites scholarly discourse.

Dear friends, by celebrating small wins—acknowledging progress, fostering resilience, nurturing optimism—we illuminate our path to success. Let us embrace each achievement, no matter how small, as a testament to our determination and dedication.

In conclusion, this chapter has explored the transformative journey of overcoming fear and taking decisive action.

Conclusion: Embracing Failure for a Resilient Future

Dear friends,

As we conclude our journey through the transformative exploration of embracing failure, let us reflect on the profound lessons learned, the resilience cultivated, and the vision for a future defined by courage, growth, and unwavering determination.

A Vision for the Future

Imagine a future where setbacks are not stumbling blocks but stepping stones to greatness. Envision a path illuminated by resilience, where each challenge navigated strengthens your spirit and propels you towards your aspirations. As we embark on this journey together, here are practical insights to help you maintain resilience over the long term:

1. **Cultivate a Growth Mindset**:

   - Embrace challenges as opportunities for growth and learning. Adopt a mindset that views setbacks as temporary setbacks rather than permanent failures.

   - Seek continuous improvement and welcome feedback as valuable insights for personal and professional development.

2. **Nurture Self-Compassion:**
   - Practice self-compassion during times of adversity. Treat yourself with kindness, acknowledging that setbacks are part of the human experience.
   - Embrace resilience as a journey of self-discovery, where each hurdle overcome strengthens your inner resilience.

3. **Set Meaningful Goals:**
   - Establish clear, achievable goals that align with your values and aspirations. Break down larger goals into smaller, manageable steps to maintain motivation and momentum.
   - Celebrate each milestone achieved, recognizing the progress made on your journey towards success.

Practical Advice for Maintaining Resilience Over the Long Term

Resilience is not a destination but a lifelong journey of growth and self-discovery. Here's practical advice to sustain resilience over the long term:

1. **Embrace Challenges as Opportunities**:
   - View challenges as opportunities to test your resilience and expand your capabilities. Approach obstacles with a proactive mindset, seeking solutions and learning from setbacks.

- Cultivate adaptability and flexibility in your approach to challenges, embracing change as a catalyst for personal and professional growth.

2. **Build a Supportive Network:**

- Surround yourself with individuals who uplift and inspire you. Foster meaningful connections with family, friends, mentors, and peers who provide encouragement and guidance.

- Seek mentorship and coaching to gain insights from experienced individuals who have navigated similar challenges and achieved success.

3. **Practice Resilience-Building Habits:**

- Incorporate daily practices that promote resilience, such as mindfulness meditation, physical exercise, and gratitude journaling.

- Prioritize self-care and well-being, ensuring you recharge and rejuvenate amidst life's demands.

Final Thoughts

Dear friends, as we part ways, let us carry with us the wisdom gained from embracing failure as a catalyst for growth and success. Remember, every setback is a lesson, and every challenge is an opportunity to discover your inner strength. Here are some final thoughts to guide you on your journey:

1. **Embrace the Journey of Growth**:
   - Embrace failure as a necessary component of the journey towards personal and professional growth. Each experience—whether triumphant or challenging—contributes to your resilience and wisdom.
   - Trust in your ability to overcome obstacles and adapt to changing circumstances. Believe in your potential to achieve greatness, guided by perseverance and determination.

2. **Celebrate Your Resilience:**
   - Celebrate the resilience you have cultivated along the way. Acknowledge your courage in facing adversity with grace and resilience, recognizing the strength within you.
   - Honor your journey of self-discovery and growth, appreciating the lessons learned and the milestones achieved.

3. **Inspire Others Through Your Story:**
   - Share your experiences of overcoming failure and embracing resilience with others. Your story has the power to inspire and encourage individuals facing similar challenges.
   - Pay it forward by supporting and uplifting those around you, fostering a community of resilience and empowerment.

Reiterating the Importance of Embracing Failure on the Path to Success

Dear friends, in our pursuit of success, let us not shy away from failure but embrace it as a transformative teacher. Failure challenges us to innovate, adapt, and persevere, paving the way for greater achievements. As we navigate life's challenges, remember:

- **Failure Strengthens Resilience**: Each setback builds resilience, equipping you with the courage and fortitude to overcome future challenges.

- **Failure Fuels Growth**: Embrace failure as an opportunity for personal and professional growth. Learn from setbacks, refine your strategies, and emerge stronger and wiser.

- **Failure Inspires Innovation**: Innovate and evolve in response to setbacks, leveraging adversity as a catalyst for creativity and innovation.

Dear friends, as you embark on your continued journey, may you embrace failure as a guiding light on the path to success. With resilience as your ally and determination as your compass, may you achieve greatness and inspire others with your unwavering spirit.

In conclusion, let us embrace failure not as an end but as a beginning—a beginning of resilience, growth, and endless possibilities. With each setback overcome, may you discover the boundless strength within you and chart a course towards a future brimming with success and fulfilment. Thank you for joining me on this transformative journey. Until we meet again, may your path be illuminated by resilience, courage, and the unwavering belief in your potential.

Warm regards!

Dear Readers,

As we conclude this transformative journey through the realms of failure, resilience, and success, I want to leave you with a resounding message—a message that echoes the heartbeat of this entire exploration: Embrace setbacks as opportunities, for within the folds of challenges lies the tapestry of unprecedented success.

In the intricate dance of life, setbacks are not roadblocks but stepping stones, not dead ends but crossroads offering new directions. Each stumble is a nudge from the universe, beckoning you to rise, learn, and propel yourself forward. It's a whisper urging you to perceive setbacks not as defeats but as invitations to unparalleled growth and achievement.

1. A Canvas for Resilience:

- *Picture setbacks as blank canvases awaiting the strokes of resilience and determination. The brush of your tenacity has the power to transform challenges into masterpieces of personal and professional triumph.*

2. Lessons in Every Setback:

- *Within setbacks lie invaluable lessons, waiting to be unearthed. Embrace the opportunity to learn, adapt, and emerge stronger. It's not about avoiding failure but about navigating it with wisdom and grace.*

3. A Symphony of Growth:

- Consider setbacks as notes in the symphony of your life. Each discordant note is an essential part of the melody, contributing to the richness of your experiences. Embrace the cacophony, for it is the prelude to a symphony of unparalleled growth.

4. Seeds of Innovation:

- Setbacks are seeds of innovation waiting to be sown. They challenge you to think differently, to explore uncharted territories, and to cultivate creativity. The fertile ground of setbacks yields the most extraordinary blooms of success.

5. Stepping Stones, Not Stumbling Blocks:

- Shift your perspective from viewing setbacks as stumbling blocks to recognizing them as stepping stones. These stones may seem uneven and challenging to traverse, but they lead to undiscovered landscapes of achievement.

6. The Phoenix's Flight:

- Like the phoenix rising from the ashes, setbacks offer the chance for a majestic rebirth. Embrace the flames of adversity, for within them lies the potential for a soaring flight to heights previously unimagined.

7. A Call to Action, Not Retreat:

- Consider setbacks as a call to action, a summons to rise and meet challenges head-on. Retreat is not an option, *for within the crucible of adversity, the steel of your resolve is forged.*

8. Fuel for Your Fire:

- Let setbacks be the fuel that stokes the fire of your ambition. They are not impediments but catalysts, igniting the flames of determination that propel you forward.

Dear readers, as you stand at the crossroads of challenges and opportunities, remember that embracing setbacks is not a sign of weakness but a testament to your courage. The path to success is not a linear one—it's a mosaic of triumphs and tribulations, setbacks and comebacks.

In the words of Winston Churchill, "Success is not final, failure is not fatal: It is the courage to continue that counts." Let the courage within you be the guiding light through the shadows of setbacks. Embrace each challenge as an opportunity to sculpt your destiny, to redefine success on your terms, and to embark on a journey where setbacks are not roadblocks but milestones marking your indomitable spirit.

So, dear reader, go forth with unwavering determination, knowing that setbacks are the raw material from which your success story is crafted. Embrace them, learn from them, and let them be the wind beneath your wings as you soar to heights beyond your wildest dreams.

References

Duckworth, A. (2016). *Grit: The Power of Passion and Perseverance.* Scribner.

Dweck, C. S. (2006). *Mindset: The New Psychology of Success.* Ballantine Books.

Brown, B. (2012). *Daring Greatly: How the Courage to Be Vulnerable Transforms the Way We Live, Love, Parent, and Lead.* Avery.

Seligman, M. E. P. (1998). *Learned Optimism: How to Change Your Mind and Your Life.* Vintage Books.

Csikszentmihalyi, M. (1990). *Flow: The Psychology of Optimal Experience.* Harper & Row.

Grant, A. (2013). *Give and Take: Why Helping Others Drives Our Success.* Penguin Books.

Kahneman, D. (2011). *Thinking, Fast and Slow.* Farrar, Straus and Giroux.

Covey, S. R. (1989). *The 7 Habits of Highly Effective People: Powerful Lessons in Personal Change.* Free Press.

Sincero, J. (2013). *You Are a Badass: How to Stop Doubting Your Greatness and Start Living an Awesome Life.* Running Press.

Gilbert, D. (2007). *Stumbling on Happiness.* Vintage Books.

Heath, C., & Heath, D. (2010). *Switch: How to Change Things When Change Is Hard.* Crown Publishing Group.

Pink, D. H. (2009). *Drive: The Surprising Truth About What Motivates Us.* Riverhead Books.

Newport, C. (2016). *Deep Work: Rules for Focused Success in a Distracted World.* Grand Central Publishing.

Goleman, D. (1995). *Emotional Intelligence: Why It Can Matter More Than IQ.* Bantam Books.

Grit, R. (2016). *The Power of Passion and Perseverance.*

Disclaimer

This book is for entertainment purposes only. Readers acknowledge that the author does not render legal, financial, medical, or professional advice. The content within this book has been derived from various sources. Please consult a licensed professional before attempting any techniques outlined in this book.

By reading this document, the reader agrees that under no circumstances is the author responsible for any direct or indirect losses incurred as a result of the use of the information contained within this document, including but not limited to errors, omissions, or inaccuracies. Adherence to all applicable laws and regulations, including international, federal, state, and local governing professional licensing, business practices, advertising, and all other jurisdictions, is the sole responsibility of the purchaser or reader. Neither the author nor the publisher assumes any responsibility or liability whatsoever on behalf of the purchaser or reader of these materials. Any perceived slight of any individual or organization is purely unintentional.

About the Author

Mahuya Gupta (B.Sc, B.Tech, M.Sc Engg, MBA), the author of "Secrets to Leverage The Power of Focus," is a dynamic professional whose career has traversed diverse realms. With a background in Applied Physics and Engineering, she honed her skills in the corporate arena, progressing from an entry-level position to a senior management role within a renowned multinational corporation in India.

A passion for writing kindled in her school days has always burned brightly within her, earning the admiration of her teachers. Although this creative pursuit took a backseat during her higher education and corporate journey, it is now rekindled with vigor through this book.

Mahuya's writing is informed by extensive research and a wealth of knowledge accumulated over her 20+ years in the corporate world. Beyond her literary endeavors, Mahuya is a multi-talented artist, proficient in various mediums of painting and a skilled violinist, with a trove of accolades garnered during her academic journey.

She can be contacted at authormahuya@gmail.com, inviting readers to engage in meaningful conversations about focus, creativity, and her diverse passions.

May I Ask You For A Small Favor?

First, I want to thank you for taking the time to read this book. You could have chosen any other book, but you took mine, and I totally appreciate this.

I hope you got at least a few actionable insights that will have a positive impact on your day-to-day life.

Can I ask for 30 seconds more of your time?

I'd love it if you could leave a review about the book. Reviews may not matter to big-name authors, but they're a tremendous help for authors like me, who don't have much following. They help me to grow my readership by encouraging folks to take a chance on my books.

To put it straight - reviews are the lifeblood of any author. Kindly visit the store where you bought this book to provide your valuable review. It will just take less than a minute of your time, but it will tremendously help me to reach out to more people, so please leave your review. Thanks for your support of my work. And I'd love to see your review.

Other Books Written By The Author

Click here to buy

Click here to buy

Click here to buy

www.ingramcontent.com/pod-product-compliance
Lightning Source LLC
Chambersburg PA
CBHW071835210526
45479CB00001B/153